PERSONAL PRAYERS
FOR TEENS

PERSONAL PRAYERS FOR TEENS

Brief meditations and prayers
dealing with experiences
common to teenagers

MIKE GRIEGER

DIMENSIONS
FOR LIVING
NASHVILLE

PERSONAL PRAYERS FOR TEENS

Library of Congress Cataloging-in-Publication Data

Grieger, Mike.
    Personal prayers for teens / Mike Grieger.
        p. cm.
    ISBN 0-687-09917-X (alk. paper)
    1. Teenagers—Prayer-books and devotions—English. I. Title.

BV4850. G73 2001
242'.83—dc21

2001032431

01 02 03 04 05 06 07 08 09 10 — 10 9 8 7 6 5 4 3 2 1

MANUFACTURED IN THE UNITED STATES OF AMERICA

THE GOOD BOOK

I have used it for just about everything: I've squashed bugs and other crawly things with it, stood on it (with others) to reach the top shelf, used it as a press when sticking things together; and it's quite a useful bookend. My dad has even borrowed it—to raise the front of the slide projector when he was showing their vacation trip for about the 80th time.

I even took it with me to church once. And I have occasionally looked inside it, as well—even if only briefly. Can this Bible I own really be the "Book of Life"? Why then do I find it so hard to get into it? Deep down I know it is God's Word; I know there is something very good inside.

At first I decided that I must have a couple of devils sitting on the cover of my Bible, making it hard for me to open. But, no, I can't put the blame on someone else.

Dear God, why do I find it so hard to get into the Bible you gave me? Help me by your Holy Spirit to dig into your Word. Let all the action, the love, and the truths make it the most exciting book in my life. Amen.

In Control

Some things really amaze me. We human beings have really come a long way—medical advances, computers, lasers, turbo engines, space travel, and all. Where else will it get to?

But then I come down to earth, and know that we have to keep things in proper focus. For example, I don't think that a scientist will ever be able to make an eye—I mean, an eye which is actually able to see. They've made glasses and contact lenses and laser surgery that can improve and correct sight, and maybe eye transplants will soon be around, but I think they might have a problem in making an eye that can see.

I sometimes think that human beings have just about everything licked. But when I think about that eye, the wonder of God and his power and absolute greatness come through. And, as one of God's family through Jesus, I feel comfortable.

Thank you, God, for reminding me that you are still in control. That makes me happy because Jesus has made me your child. Help me to see the many, many wonderful things that show me that you are truly the Lord of all, the creator of all. Amen.

CLEAN INSIDE

The circle in the schoolyard was getting bigger. At first there had been just a few, but little by little others got curious and began to crowd around.

It got to me, too. Standing on tiptoe, craning the neck, pushing and stretching, leaning over others' shoulders, I eventually got a look. It was one of those magazines—you know, the ones that leave nothing to imagination.

For a while, I was tugged in two directions. I was interested, all right, and sort of enjoyed what I saw—but I also felt uncomfortable. Obviously, most in the group thought it great, and were excited over the pictures. But I got the nagging twinge in the back of my mind. That made me angry at first, but then I was thankful.

Thank you, Lord, for a conscience that is alive. Help me to listen to it when you and your Word are behind it. I knew what we were doing was not right, was not giving glory to you. Forgive me, and keep my mind and conscience clean, for Jesus' sake. Amen.

CARE AND CURE

I don't get sick very often, but just at present I feel lousy. It's so bad that even my skin hurts. It's as if my head is all filled up with hot water and someone has me in a headlock, trying to squeeze it all out. My eyes are bulging, my nose running, my ears close to exploding. I try to get relief by drinking fluids, but that stings too as it runs down my tight and tender throat. I think I have a cold.

The worst thing is: *I* have the cold. It's *mine,* no one else's. I'm alone in all this misery. I can't give my pain to anyone else—and I don't think they care, anyhow. I even catch myself wondering whether God cares and knows how I feel.

I sure must be a real big pain to those around me. Mom says that there are always others worse off, and that I'm just making things worse by feeling sorry for myself. I guess I am!

Help me, Jesus, to understand what illness can do to me; help me to look beyond myself. I'm counting on you, dear Lord, for help, forgiveness, patience, and getting well again. Soon, please. Amen.

GETTING IT RIGHT

Life seems to be ruled by so many don'ts, by the possibility of "the sick" at the end of the action. The list is endless: Don't be promiscuous or you might catch AIDS, Don't drink and drive; you might lose your license or your life, Don't smoke; it can lead to cancer, heart disease, and the grave, Don't take drugs; they will kill your brain first, and then you yourself.

Even good old-fashioned eating gets the ax: Don't eat fatty foods, salty foods, sugary foods, take-out foods; if you do, all sorts of strange-sounding medical monsters will get you in the end.

So it goes on—even with lesser things. We end up shaping our behavior by the consequences, not by the action itself. We end up being motivated by results, not by what is right or godly.

Jesus, be my master, and rule my life by your love. Teach me to do the positive things that are pleasing to you. That way, I'll get it right with your help. And then I'll be doing the do's, and won't need to be concerned about the don'ts. Amen.

FRUITFUL LIVING

Evangelism: it's never been my type of word. It's a word that's had no claim on me; I thought it belonged to others—particularly others in the church. It even sounded complicated and off-putting—something older people talk about a lot. If ever anything was to be done about the word, it sure needn't involve me.

But, scratching around in my Bible a few days ago, I came across some words which set me thinking: "You did not choose me; I chose you . . . to go and bear much fruit, the kind of fruit that endures" (John 15:16 TEV). That made me feel special—I belong to Jesus because he chose me.

But it jolted me, too. I realized that being a Christian isn't all getting; it involves a job to be done. Jesus chooses you and me for a purpose. Now I'm starting to learn how evangelism also fits into all that. It is sharing Jesus with others.

Lord, I can't understand how you ever chose a person like me—but you did, and I'm glad. You hung on to me even when I was slow to respond. I didn't even like the sound of the word evangelism, *let alone do something about it. Help me to bear enduring fruit for you, Lord, by being a friend to others and by sharing you, my Friend, with them. Amen.*

Controlled Speaking

I'm still not sure what really happened. I simply made a few statements based on what I saw to be the facts, and then some conclusions I drew from those facts. To my mind, I was telling it just as it was. But wow! What a storm!

Why is it that I am so misunderstood? I wasn't trying to hurt anyone or mislead anyone. And I had no ulterior motives when I said what I did. And now it's come back to me all wrong. I've been accused of saying things that I never said at all.

Good communicating is really hard. Obviously, you have to be careful not just in what you say, but in how it is understood and received.

Forgive me, Jesus, if I have said things that are wrong or hurtful. Help me to be a good communicator, saying things carefully, truthfully, and lovingly, not only with my words but also in my body language and attitude of heart. Help me to be a good listener, too, so that I do not understand others. Help me to be loving, open, and kind. Amen.

"I LOVE YOU"

When I was little, I used to find it so easy to say: "I love you." I could say it to Mom and Dad, to others in my family, and even to my best friends at school and church.

But that now seems all changed. Now that I'm older, it's not only that I can't say it; I even get embarrassed just *thinking about* saying it. And the strange thing is that the closer that people are to me, the harder it is for me to get it out.

I know by their actions that my parents love me (well, most of the time); but I also know how good it feels when they actually say to me: "I love you."

Please help me, Lord, to say "I love you" to my parents and to others close to me. Actions of love are good, but not enough. Help me to give my loved ones the same warm feeling of love that those words give me. Help me to say them this very day.

And, Jesus, I love you, too. Amen.

MAKING THINGS RIGHT

I feel terrible. I did something wrong today, and the shame and guilt of it all won't go away. I wish it hadn't happened, that I hadn't done it, that I could set things right as they were before—but all that is now too late.

I thought up excuses which I could make for my action. I even thought up some good lies as reasons for what I did. I also tried to blame anybody else but me. All that helped for a while, but it wasn't long before the nagging guilt came back.

The memory fills my mind, and it hurts. I want forgiveness; but I also want to run away from the embarrassment of saying I was wrong and of asking how I can put things right.

Heavenly Lord, please forgive me for Jesus' sake; I know I have sinned, and I first need to hear your word of pardoning love. But then help me to face the music by admitting my wrong, saying I'm sorry, and trying to make things right. And help me to avoid making that mistake again. Fill my life again with joy and peace. Amen.

NOT FORGOTTEN

She was sort of all crunched up, wrinkled, with whispy gray hair, eyes rather lifeless peering almost vacantly over her glasses (one wing of which was sitting on the wrong side of the ear).

The sight made me angry and hateful of old age. And it also made me scared, for I suddenly realized that one day I could end up like that, too—if God lets my life last that long. I, too, could be old, useless—perhaps even forgotten.

As she wobbled her way toward me, I wondered if she had once been beautiful. But then I knew. She lifted her gray head, and her cracked lips parted to show a few worn and weary teeth as she smiled. Though she could no longer give much, her smile gave all she had—with cheerfulness and inner beauty.

Lord, help me to understand older people, to respect them, and to help and care for them where I can. You made them to be older when I am young. Make me open to whatever they can give me, and vice versa. Amen.

IMPORTANT AND NOTICED

She stood there so smugly, slouching against the classroom door, exaggerating her figure in a most annoying way. She didn't really need to flaunt her assets in such an arrogant manner. Show-off, I thought! What really made me angry was the way she succeeded in grabbing and keeping the attention of others.

But that's when I came to realize that I really can't talk. In my own way, *I* have been doing the same thing. Of course, my ways have been less obvious, more subtle, but I've been trying to get other people to notice me, too.

But now I wonder: Are my ways really so subtle? Perhaps they are as obvious to others as that girl's efforts were to me. I've also been trying to get noticed by outward appearance or bizarre behavior.

Jesus, I do want to be recognized; I do need to feel important. But help me to meet that need in the right way. First, remind me how important I am to you, no matter how I dress or look. And then help me to be noticed because of my Christian personality, caring, sharing, helping. Amen.

Counting my blessings

It's the pits in our house; they're always at me. "Pick up your clothes. Stop your fighting. Do your homework. Tidy up your room. Help with the dishes!" It's all nag-nag-nag.

Why can't they leave me alone? Sometimes I just don't seem to do anything right—I certainly often don't *feel* like doing it. Sometimes it seems that God provided parents just to even out things with the good things I have in my life. When I'm enjoying something, sure enough they come along and wreck it. They insist that they love me, and that they're doing all this nagging for my benefit, but it's often hard to see how.

Actually, when I stop to think about it, I don't really mean all I've just said. I guess my parents are always there when I need to count on them. I mean, deep down I know they do care. When *I* don't care about something, I just don't bother; but Mom and Dad are always bothered about me. I think that must be a good sign.

God in heaven, help my parents to understand me, and help me to understand them, too. Amen.

Hair is in!

My hair today just wouldn't go where it was supposed to; it just wouldn't sit straight.

Normally, I have no problems with it, but today of all days I can't do a thing with it. A bit is sticking up here in the front, the back ended up as an utter disaster, and the part that I plastered down with water looks absolutely gross.

My hair is important to me. It's a large part of the way people see me. I mean: Hair is in! How can people like me when my hair is like it is today?

Dear God, please help me to look good. I know you want me to be less concerned with the outside, and more with the inside—my heart, and all that. And I do need you to give attention to my inside. But right now, God, I do need some help with my hair. What can I do? Show me, Lord. Amen.

Hear my prayer

Why is it that I don't feel like praying tonight? It's not that I really don't *want* to; it's just that I've had such a terrific time out tonight, and now I'm *so* tired. And it's quite late, too. I'm finding it hard to concentrate on thinking the right thoughts and putting the right words together—at least, putting words together in a prayer that makes any sense.

Jesus, I remember how tired you must have been in the Garden that night before you died for me. And yet, all you did was to pray—and perspire blood with the anguish and the strain. If only I were like you.

Would it be OK if I just said the Lord's Prayer tonight—and leave longer prayers to when I can think of what to say next? Or can your Spirit pray the words for me, like the Bible says?

I'll catch you in the morning, Lord. Be with me again through this night. Amen.

A GREAT WEEKEND!

Wow! What a great weekend I've had! I lazed about all Saturday morning, and then we won our game on Saturday afternoon. To top it off, there was the terrific time with my friends at night. On Sunday, after church, the gang all went down to the beach. The weather was fantastic, and we all had a ball.

Isn't it great when you have friends to enjoy life with! If I had no one to share fun with, it wouldn't be half as good!

Thank you, Lord, for the joy of this past weekend, and for all the many other good times I have had that were just like it. Thank you for giving me the time to enjoy myself and the freedom to choose what I want to do. And thank you again for good friends. Amen.

Needs and Wants

It's not fair! All around our house all I ever hear is: "We can't afford that. It costs too much. Do you think money grows on trees?"

What a stupid question! Why don't Mom and Dad understand how I feel? I mean, most of the other kids in school get whatever they want whenever they feel like it. I'm told either that I have to wait, or that the thing I want is just beyond the budget. It's just my luck to wind up in a poor family!

God, when I think about it, I guess I do have all I need—I mean, really need. First, I have you, and all the blessings Jesus won for me on the cross. And then I have Mom and Dad and a comfortable home and friends at school and church. And enough to eat—and Mom's reasonable cooking. So I ought to be satisfied.

Dear God, please give me wisdom to know the difference between what I need and what I want. Amen.

Making it Specific

In my prayers I do say: "And help all the starving people in the world, and bless them with what they need," but it all seems so distant and unreal to me. I really struggle with that type of prayer. I want to have real meaning and feeling in my heart for such people, but the problem is so enormous, so repeated, so widespread that it's hard to picture specific people or specific needs.

I really want to help, to be able to do something, but I always seem to end up with a vague, general prayer—and little action to follow.

Lord, help me to narrow it down. Help me to think about one needy kid. I don't know why, but that always ends up as a tiny child with no hair, ribs protruding, mishapen stomach, and big sad eyes, scared and in pain, not knowing why she has to be hungry, or how she will get her next meal—and not even caring what is served up, as long as it's food. Why is it that she is hungry and not me?

Dear Lord, give that poor anonymous child your full love and care. The problem of hunger is too big for me to understand. But I do care. Please help me from now on to care even more, and to do even more to help out, giving so that it hurts. Amen.

OH, WHAT A FEELING!

I feel great: People are giving me more and more responsibilities. My parents are trusting me with more important things, and letting me make more decisions. My teachers expect more from me now— and the older people I know seem to believe that I can cope with more difficult situations.

I like that feeling. I like it that I'm getting more capable. I feel proud of myself.

Help me, Dear God, to handle my increased responsibilities, so that I do not let down the people who are trusting me. Keep me willing to listen, willing to learn how I can do things better. Help me to be open to advice when it is given, even if I tend to disagree at the time. Give me patience and maturity, and the ability to think things through—and especially to discover what Jesus my Savior would do in my situation. Amen.

Taking time to see

Scratching around in the garden the other day, I disturbed a worm. I'd never really stopped to have a close look at a worm before. There it was, stretching and shrinking its solf vulnerable body, squirming and wriggling in an urgent effort to cover itself again with the warm soil, and to flee from me, the disturber.

As I peered down on hands and knees, so close to the ground, I smelled the rich soil. As the worm gave the last flick of its rear end and was gone, I was left to stare fascinated at the little crumbles of dirt: multicolored grains of this and that, all sorts of elements compounded together, I guess.

Thank you, heavenly Lord, for the beauty, the wonder, the mystery of creation. We often close our eyes to it or take it so much for granted. Help me as your child to look after your creation, and to take time to appreciate the many wonders which surround us. Amen.

CONFRONTING DEATH

It was all rather scary. I had known this person at church just a little. The last time I had greeted her, she was alive. But now, before me was her life-less shell, lying in the rich dark timber of her coffin and surrounded by the usual smell of roses. It was my first funeral; for the first time in my life I con-fronted the fact that death is so final.

I secretly would have liked to touch the body to feel the coldness, to touch the reality of death—but I presumed that that isn't done. And, besides, I was a little scared.

Should I have been scared, Lord? I suppose I shouldn't. Bring me to know the full Christian hope in the face of death, to rejoice like Paul, "Where, Death, is your victory? Where, Death, is your power to hurt?"

I am so full of living that I hardly ever stop to think of dying. Help me to face the reality of death; but even more, give me the assurance that, because you died for me, I have nothing to fear, and that after my death I will wake up in heaven to be with you forever. Amen.

ENJOYING SPORTS

Sports are great fun; I really enjoy it. It's great to feel part of a team. And it's terrific to be able to say that we've won—even when I didn't contribute all that much to the win. It's even better when I do, and can look with pride on the goal I kicked/threw, the catch or the winning shot I made.

Sports have many advantages. Competition helps to develop my skills, and gets the adrenalin flowing. It gives me lots of friends and can teach me all sorts of lessons for life. And if we make the finals, the happiness and excitement is a bonus.

Help me to be a good sport, dear Lord. Help me to win graciously when we win, and to lose graciously when we lose—even though that's hard sometimes. Help me to be honest and fair whenever I compete, and to accept defeats and decisions that go against us. Teach me that it's better to lose honestly than to win by wrong means. Thank you for the skills I have; help me to improve them, and to play even better. Amen.

Needing Glasses

None of my friends know it yet, but I've just learned that I need glasses. Can you imagine it: glasses for my eyes! Yuck!

I don't suppose I should, but I've always looked on the wearing of glasses as a sign of weakness—just like braces to straighten teeth, neck collars, and hearing aids. They're certainly not cool, anyhow. A broken arm is different; it's OK because all the kids hang around to ask about it.

Now, of course, the shoe's on the other foot. *I'm* the one who has to have them. Will others look down on me? With glasses, I'll certainly look different. I hope my friends don't laugh too much.

Why is it, Lord, that it takes something like this to make me think about others? Is that why you gave me poor eyes? I'm starting to realize what others in this situation must feel, whereas I've never stopped to consider their feelings before. Help me to be sensitive and understanding about the weaknesses and embarrassments of other people. Don't let such things influence the way I treat people. And I hope my glasses won't change the way people treat me. Amen.

PUTTING THINGS OFF

I was called a new name today: *Procrastinator* (I think that's how it's spelled). Well, kids my age have been called all sorts of things: rebellious, difficult, stubborn, self-willed, assertive, immature—and lots of others, which I needn't list because you've probably heard them all before. But this new word grabs me because it describes me to a T—most of the time I *do* put things off.

Why is it so hard to come to grips with things, to make decisions? It's so easy to put things off—not only homework and stuff like that which comes to mind just now, but all sorts of other unpleasant or difficult things. I continually put things off "for an hour," or I leave it "till later." The trouble is, putting things off rarely makes it easier.

Help me, Lord, to stop procrastinating—especially in the important things of life. As I'm growing up and developing, build into my life the ability to do things right away.

Most of all, Lord, stop me from putting off the things that concern my relationship with you. You did not hesitate to face the cross for me; help me to act strongly and promptly to keep my faith in you strong, and growing, and permanent. Amen.

Sucked in by swearing

At first I managed to hold it back. But then suddenly it all poured out. I swore—not just a few mild efforts (as if that is ever excused), but some real beauties, a real explosion of profanity.

In my weakness, I really got caught up in all the excitement of the moment. I wanted to prove to the rest of the gang that I was no different from them. I wanted to be like them and to be accepted by them. I didn't want to be thought of, or sneered at, as a goody-goody. So swearing seemed quite in order, the normal and accepted thing to do.

The worst of all was that it didn't bother me; I didn't think anymore about it until long afterward.

I must be weak, dear Jesus, to get sucked in like that. Please forgive me; I know what I did was wrong. Help me to get on top of this weakness; you take over my life so that what I say is always pure and pleasing to you. I really need your help on this one, Lord. Amen.

IF ONLY I COULD!

Nothing's gone right for me at school today. And it all started with my troubles in computer studies. I was slow at solving the problem right from the start, and I got frustrated. I just couldn't get the program for a delivery van schedule to work. So I ended up being last to key in the data—and everybody noticed it.

So I missed recess. Then afterward the teacher said what I'd done was wrong—and I'd have to stay after school to do it again. And everybody heard that, too.

Imagine how frustrated and depressed I feel, dear God. You were lucky, Jesus; you didn't have computers and complicated problems like that when you were at school. But you could have done them—easily. Please help me with my schoolwork—especially this dumb computer stuff. Amen.

Stupid Drugs

You certainly can't escape talk about drugs these days, but the real message coming through isn't pretty. I have no wish to ever try them.

Some of my friends at school say they have tried them. They reckon they know where to go for a fix or to get a joint. Half the time I don't believe them; I'm sure they just want to show off in front of the rest of us.

The truth is, getting involved in drugs is pretty stupid. I also know that I'm not doing enough to fight them. I say to myself that it's not my scene, and that if others want to be stupid, let them kill themselves. But I'm sure that's not the right way to tackle this.

Thank you, God, for keeping me free from drugs. Please see to it that it stays that way. And keep me free from being smug. Help me to help those who think they need them. Amen.

TEACH ME TO PRAY

Well, I decided to start using the prayerbook that was given to me. Some pages were good, but most of the time I seemed to get little help for my praying.

Actually, I do find it hard to really pray. Sometimes—well, quite often—I have the feeling that praying is artificial, unreal. You know, fold your hands, close your eyes, bow your head, and God will be there to hear your thoughts and words. I do that in church, but so often the words seem empty and leave me unmoved. And often at the end of the day, when my body says: "Go to sleep," the prayer I just managed to squeeze in often seems a bit shallow.

Dear Lord, draw me closer to you as my Savior and friend, and then teach me to pray. Give me the excitement of real heart-to-heart talks with you. Amen.

Sunday after Sunday

I've been really struggling to understand why I should go to church Sunday after Sunday. But I sure got a new point of view on that today.

I was told that, humanly speaking, it's a lot like joining a gym or a fitness club. If you are going to get the benefit of all the blessings the club offers, you have to make the commitment to go regularly. That way, you get the benefits by participating, practicing, being part of the team, and you at the same time enthuse others.

To be part of God's family or team works the same way—but, of course, on a much higher level.

Lord, I really want to be on your team. And you have so many blessings to give me through your Word. Help me to want those through weekly worship, and to be there for others. Amen.

Enjoying wrong

What is wrong with me? I do want to be a Christian and to belong to God, but so often I find myself really enjoying some things that are wrong.

The more I examine my life, the more I find examples of where I have actually enjoyed sinning—and sometimes I've even planned such opportunities. I surely must be either very weak or very sinful. Can I really be a Christian while this is going on?

Thank goodness, I have been taught the answer to that. Being a Christian doesn't depend on what I do, but on what Jesus has done for me. But I still feel ashamed at the way I behave sometimes.

Jesus, forgive me for giving in to my favorite sins. No matter how big my sins, your salvation is bigger. But make my faith better and stronger so that I can cleanse my conduct and overcome my sinful tendencies. I don't want to drive those nails into your hands even more deeply. Amen.

GROWING IS SO SLOW!

It's no fun the way the girls keep looking me up and down. I can see they are comparing my smooth, hairless legs with the hairy ones of other guys. I know they are putting me down, inwardly snickering because I seem so immature—light years away from puberty.

That makes me feel so low. They say it's all part of growing up—but that doesn't make it any easier. One day I'll show 'em—but I wish it wouldn't take so long.

I'm really struggling inside, God, and hurting. I wish people would be more thoughtful and kind. I know I'm growing up, but it's taking so long. Help me to be patient, and help others to be more understanding. It's good to know you must understand, Jesus, because you were once a teenager at Nazareth. Amen.

Family frustration

I'm really worked up and angry. Most of my friends would have gone to the game today, and the rest would have watched on TV—and tomorrow that's all they'll be talking about at school. How am *I* going to feel?

How can I tell them that our family went visiting the relatives, and that all they talked about was growing tomatoes and beans or pruning stupid old fruit trees?

Why did I have to go along to all that and miss all the real action?

God, I'm angry and upset. It seems as if they take pleasure in making me suffer. Help me to get over this anger, Lord. I know they love me, that they want me as part of the family, and that they want our family life to be warm and united. I do, too—but it's really tough sometimes. Amen.

Too tough for tears?

Most of the kids thought it was laughable—and I did too, before I thought again. This guy was crying—not just sniffling, but really sobbing away—and all we could do was to laugh. All we could do was to think: What a sissy! But that's the trouble: we didn't really think.

Now that I'm here alone, I keep seeing the guy in my mind, and I feel a bit cruel. I keep wondering why he was crying, and feel guilty for not even bothering to find out. I was content just to follow the crowd blindly and thoughtlessly.

And why do we keep on acting as if boys should be too tough for tears?

Forgive me my thoughtlessness, my failure to accept and understand someone's tears. Forgive me for all the times when I don't try to understand other people's feelings and needs. Amen.

A GREAT BODY

It's a great feeling under the shower: hot water sloshing all over my body; the shower turned on full blast; heaps of soap suds smoothly sliding down my legs and racing away down the drain.

But standing there and thinking about one's own naked body can be strange. There I was, wanting to tell myself how terrific and good-looking my body was, and the gremlins landed. I saw my skinny legs, my three very odd-shaped toes, my nobbly kneecaps, and my gangling arms. And that made me feel my face to remind me of the pimples ready to pop. It makes you wonder what other kids think or say about me.

But, of course, there is more to life than having a great body.

Keep working on me, Jesus, to keep up my self-esteem. I know you think I'm worth something because you died for me. Help me to love myself in the same way as you do. Then it won't really matter what others think or say—but if they think I'm OK, that will be a great bonus. Amen.

Washed clean

The dream I had was so vivid and real: I saw myself as a rag, lying in the gutter, soiled, sodden with sludge and slime. Broken glass, polluting plastic, and muck were my constant companions. I was not out of place because I was filth myself, pollution myself, and with no power or desire to change. The only action was the onflowing movement of the sludge sliding over me, pushed on by the new muck bringing up the rear.

Then a man struggled by, with scars on his hands and feet. He stooped low into the gutter and looked. He had tears in his eyes because he can never forget that time when he was anguished and pain-racked, treated like the ugliest and filthiest of rags. He stretched out a scarred hand and gently picked me up. Lovingly, he began to squeeze out the filth, washing me clean with his tears. I am clean again because he cared.

I love you, Jesus. How can I thank you for dying for me? Amen.

FACT OF FAITH

Sometimes when lying in bed at night, or at other thinking times when I am alone, these unsettling thoughts and questions nag at me: Am I being stupid when I believe in God? Is it being wise and facing reality to believe in someone/something you can't see or hear or touch? Where are you, God?

I mean, all around me, there are real things which I see and handle, there are maths and science problems where I prove the answer to be true. But I can't do that with God. I know the Bible is true, and I do want to believe its message. But I do feel a bit sheepish believing in God when so many around me scoff and sneer and consider me odd.

Dear God, it's hard to explain this feeling I have, but do you know what I mean? Help me to cope with the pressure, to grow stronger in the faith despite the nagging questions. Remind me to hang in there, to stay close to the Bible, to remember that you made me your child in Baptism; then your Holy Spirit will keep showing me that Jesus is real, salvation is real, and that faith is more lasting than the things I touch and taste. Amen.

SELFISHNESS

I've got a friend who is so selfish. She's always thinking and talking about herself.

Every morning before school starts, she asks: "How do I look?" Then she'll tell me everything she did last night, and everything she's going to do. If we want to do something, we either do what she wants, or nothing at all.

I guess I shouldn't criticize because we're all selfish in different ways. I know; I'm always thinking about myself. "What do others think of me? How can I make others like me more?" I keep thinking about and focusing on the things *I* want, the things *I* enjoy, the rights *I* have which others should recognize. Other people end up a poor second, and God comes last.

If I'm thinking about me all the time, what's worrying is that I must be a real pain for others. Selfish people must be hard to love.

Jesus, you must be able to help me; you never thought about yourself, and you changed selfish people, like Zacchaeus. Help me to be like you. Change me by giving me your kind of love. Make my first thought not for myself, but how I can please God and bring happiness to others. Amen.

Awkwardness

It's sure not easy growing up and trying to take control of things in your life. Just the other day I was feeling so confident and self-assured. I was bragging to the other kids at school about how I was going to impress this person at the dance. I had the scene perfectly planned and rehearsed: the words I would use to break the ice, how I would subtly impress in the follow-up, and finally take control. It all seemed so easy.

But it all fell to pieces. When I was two steps away from my planned opener, suddenly the blood rushed to my face and there I stood paralyzed and awkward. Brain and mouth got out of step, and the words that came out were confused and corny. So much for a good impression!

God, why did this happen to me? Why didn't it turn out as I had hoped? Is it because I'm basically shy and tried to be something other than myself? Is it because I forgot that growing up is filled with lots of ups and downs, and that your plan for my life is so often different to the one I think up. Help me to be myself. Help me to grow in courage and self-confidence. Above all, help me to take disappointments in my stride and to accept that you love me as your child, and that you are guiding my life always. Amen.

CHANGES

I don't quite know how to put this properly as I talk to you, Maker and Lord. But if it comes out awkwardly and crudely, I know you will get it right because you know what's in my heart and how I really feel.

I am excited and stirred by this new feeling in my body. I know it's got to do with my future behavior with the other sex, and that there's a right way and a wrong way to treat it. And I know the way the kids talk about it in the yard at school is a lot different from what the Bible says.

But right now I'm simply thinking about the wonder, the mystery of this new feeling, this new physical urge. And I somehow feel that how I deal with it will influence my whole future.

You gave me a wonderful body, Lord, and all these new wonderful sexual feelings. Help me understand them, to be happy about them, and to control them as the special gift that they are. Amen.

WHOM DO I FOLLOW?

It seems a contradiction to me. On the one hand, everybody these days says it's OK to do your own thing. But, if you do, that often means breaking away from the crowd. And that's not very comfortable. Who wants to be an outsider? I want to be accepted, to be part of the group.

This is where I really need your help, Lord. Many times the group I'm in wants to do things that I know are wrong: ganging up, backstabbing, urging someone to lie, stealing things, damaging or destroying things, and that sort of thing. As a group, we say that it's just for kicks, just for the heck of it, just to try ourselves out, and to see if we can get away with it. But, individually, we all know it's wrong.

But, even though I know it's wrong, I'm scared to break from the group. I know what they'd say if I did. But I know what you'd feel and say if I don't. So please help me, Lord, to be brave, and to do the right thing. I know that is best in the end. Amen.

Holidays are great

Holidays are fantastic! Now I feel free again, really free. Free from the routine, free from the boredom and sameness of each day: Get up—Go to school—Come home—Do chores and homework—Go to bed. Now it's a case of doing whatever I like: Sleep in—Go to the beach—Just hang around—Watch the late movie. If only that could go on forever!

But, of course, I know it can't. And I know I would soon be bored. And I know I would soon be looking for something more satisfying.

Thanks for holidays, Lord, and thanks for the freedom to do the things that I like, when I like. But help me to want to like things other than a lazy do-nothing-much time: helping around the house, contributing to the family, helping a neighbor out, reaching out to someone sick or lonely, helping out at church. Give me fun and a sense of satisfaction from giving of my time and freedom for others, because I belong to you. Amen.

My beautiful bed!

Of all the things I possess, there's surely nothing better than my bed. It's mine—all mine. I know I didn't buy it—my parents did—but everybody knows it's mine.

With the blankets pulled right up to my nose, it's so snug and cozy when it's wintry outside. And in summer it's great to stretch out and relax on it with just a sheet on top of me. I'm really stupid to abuse it by jumping on it, or by staying out too late at night.

If I had no bed, I guess I could get by with something much less—as countless people have to each night.

Thank you, Lord, for my bed, for the comfort of it all. But give me a heart to help the many less fortunate people with some of the plenty you've given me. Amen.

Cool Clothes

Of course, I think clothes are important. Ever since I was small, I've heard about wearing one's Sunday best to church—out of respect for God, I guess.

But it's not always good clothes that make me feel good. It's what's with it, cool, in fashion, that counts. When I wear clothes like that, I feel good—and I'm sure they help me look good, too.

Mind you, too many people judge others by outward things like clothes. But clothes should be way down the list. Far more important is what's on the inside, what people want out of life, what things they want to share with their friends, what fun they can have regardless of what they are wearing.

Jesus, help me to place importance on things that really count. Help me to judge myself and my friends on inner attitudes rather than outward appearances, on goodness of body, mind, and soul. Amen.

YOUNGER SISTER/BROTHER

I don't know whether Jesus had younger sisters or brothers, but *I* sure have. One of each—and they're both real pains. Particularly the one who's about two years younger than I am. They want everything I've got, stick their nose into all my stuff, and make me really embarrassed especially when my friends are around. When I want to do something special, they are sure to hang around like a bad smell. When I ask them to get lost, they go squealing to Mom or Dad—and guess what happens then!

Help my younger brother and sister, Jesus, to understand that I do love them, but that there are times when I just don't want them around. And, of course, help me to understand that they hang around because they love me and want to grow up and learn by being with older company and doing older things. Help all in our family to stay close to each other in love both when we are together and when we are by ourselves. Amen.

Hang in there!

"Hang in there," they said. "Stick it out—and you'll eventually see that it will all be worth it." But I'm not convinced—even though they say they've been through the same pressures and know how I feel.

I'm often tempted to think this commitment business is all just a big bluff. You know, commitment to study, commitment to training, commitment to one's job, to being good, to being a true friend. I sometimes feel like rebelling, so that the only thing worth committing myself to is: doing nothing.

And then there's that phrase heard so often that So-and-so is "a committed Christian." How do you get to be such a Christian? Is there such a thing as an uncommitted Christian?

Lord God, to be a Christian is the most important thing in my life. But I can't get the commitment for that by myself; I need your Holy Spirit. Amen.

JUST AS I AM

Life is so full of downs and doubts, fears and frustrations, pains and problems. I know I'm not the worst off in the world, but my life has plenty. But when I think about all this, I reckon I have one most important concern: to be accepted.

I want to be accepted for who I am, to be accepted just as I am, to be accepted for my own sake. To be accepted without conditions by those around me who really count—my friends, my pastor and church friends, and especially my folks.

Jesus, you surely know how I feel. For a while you had things going OK. You had your twelve disciples and other followers, and the Palm Sunday crowd shouting and waving branches accepting you as their king. But when the crunch came, and you needed them most, they were not around; all you could cling to was your Father. When people let me down, and I feel alone, let me know that you are still there, that I am not just accepted, but fully acceptable because of Calvary. I know you have higher hopes for me, and I'm trying to fulfill them because you have already accepted me. Amen.

GROWING UP

It looked simple enough on TV—and when my folks used it, too: Shake the can like mad, lift up your arm, and squirt. But the first time I tried it, I missed my underarm completely and zonked the mirror; the next time it was the side of my face. But when I finally got the hang of it, I felt really good; I felt I was grown-up at last. The stuff had a real grown-up smell about it.

I wish growing up was as easy as that: a squirt here, a squirt there, and it's all instantly OK for now. But I know it isn't like that.

God, I know that growing up takes time, and that I need time to listen, to learn, to understand, to recover from mistakes, to mature. Give me patience. Help me to enjoy my growing up despite my many embarrassments, and give me joy when I make right decisions. Be my guide, Lord, and help me to understand that I'm in a growing period that's shaping my whole life. Above all, help me grow in my faith. Amen.

Facing my faults

Heavenly Lord, today was no different—I've been guilty of doing many wrong things. Please forgive me because of Jesus who died in my place.

In a way, it seems fairly easy to ask for forgiveness from you—because I don't have to physically look you in the eye. It seems a lot harder to say I'm sorry to Mom or Dad, or to apologize to someone at school, when they are standing right in front of you.

But really, God, you are always in front of me—in fact, all around me, and your Spirit dwells in me. So, help me to face up to my sins more wisely. I know you already know them, but help me to know them properly by confessing them, and naming each one that I can recall. I am truly sorry for all my bad ways, for all the things I do that put me out of step with you. Thank you for Jesus, for daily forgiveness, and for the gift of a new day to make a new start. Amen.

LIFE AS IT IS

When I'm absolutely starving and a long way from home on a hot day, it's so easy to dream of tasty delights in the fridge: ice-cold soft drinks or delicious raspberry sherbet; all the makings for a cheese-and-pickle or ham-and-pineapple sandwich; leftover cold chicken with the spicy, crispy skin still intact; more than one slice of chocolate cake or meringue pie—even my favorite cake from last night's dinner.

But the reality rarely turns out that way. I come home ravenous and open the fridge door—and it's almost empty: A few wrinkled apples (and even the green kind), a dish of burned fried tomatoes, and some unappetizing leftover leathery toast. I'm angry as well as hungry—and Mom gets the blame.

Hang on! Mom's not to blame; I am. I had the exaggerated dreams; I was the one who caused my let-down. Lord, help me to think straight and to meet life as it really is. So, thanks for all the wonderful food and drink that my parents and the fridge have given me. Amen.

CARING COUSINS

We visited some relatives yesterday, and at the table the adults began discussing a family problem. It was one of my cousins. I didn't catch on to all the details—but, believe me, what I heard was enough! And something *I'd* never do!

So I can't wait until I see my other cousins to talk about it. I'll feel so important and grown-up; they'll think I'm really smart knowing such juicy stuff. I won't mention names, of course, but they'll probably work out who it is, anyhow.

But—what if it were me they were talking about behind my back? I wouldn't feel good knowing my cousins were spreading my wrongs around.

Lord, help me to keep my mouth shut at times like that. Forgive me for feeling smug about the mistakes of others, and for getting joy out of hurting others. Make my heart and tongue clean. Amen.

Hanging back

It's not easy always pitching in when others expect or want you to. I'm often told that one of my favorite sayings is the line: "I don't feel like it." Sometimes I just hate that word *participate*—when I'd much rather hang back, watch from the last row, or disappear completely from the scene of the action.

I guess I don't like the idea that others will be watching me, and will surely laugh at me because I'll show how dumb I really am. I suppose most of the time I worry too much about what others think. And maybe I imagine that they are watching me like a hawk when they're too busy with their own participation and effort.

I guess I just need lots of encouragement, and need to respond to the encouragement my parents, teachers, youth leader, and friends are already giving.

Help me, Jesus, to get rid of my tendency to hang back, so that I can enjoy participating with the group. I'm sure you will see to it that I have fun and learn from every experience. Amen.

EARLY TO BED

It happened again! Just as I was getting organized to do something, my parents told me to go to bed. Don't they understand that I'm old enough to make decisions myself? My friends' parents let them stay up much later than I ever can; it's a real pain. I can't wait for when they get off my back and let me decide for myself. It's almost as if I've been sent to bed so that I'm out of their hair. It's not fair!

Anyhow, beds are for when you're sick or deadbeat—and that's not too often! Or a place to think—and I'm not really in the mood for thinking just now.

But here I am in bed. I'm not sick, and I'm definitely not tired, so thinking is all I can do. Maybe I'm the one who's not fair? Maybe it would be worse if my parents didn't care, didn't love me, didn't bother whether or when I went to sleep?

Lord, help me to appreciate my parents, to try to see their point of view when it clashes with my plans. Give us a warm and good relationship. Help me to play my part so that hopefully they will learn to trust me and even let me stay up later sometimes.

You know, I'm starting to feel glad they sent me to bed; it's given me a longer quiet time for talking to you. Amen.

What shall I be?

We had a career counselor at school today, and each one of us in the class was given a careers booklet. It sure got a lot of us interested. Some of us got together after school, and sat around to go through the booklet again. Page by page we read it, telling each other which of the jobs we were interested in (I had ten). All looked to be good, pleasant jobs that paid lots of money.

After I left the group, and set out for home, I kept thinking about how we were measuring possible future jobs, and suddenly it hit me. Fame, status, money, chance of promotion, expenses-paid trips, and things like that were the important things— what the job would give me, not what I could give to the job or how I could help others. New thoughts like those make the decision a lot harder.

Dear Lord, I'm growing up, and my life is starting to take shape. But since I'm not too sure how it is shaping, help me to depend on you. Help me with my schoolwork and study. Guide me to make right decisions about a career. Help me to find a job, which will require not only my education and skills but also my Christian faith and my care and concern for others. Amen.

It's so easy

My parents always taught me to be honest. I can still feel from many years ago the "encouragement" I got when I took some coins from my Mom's purse. But no worries! I'm in favor of honesty, and I can't see why kids can brag about stealing things from the local supermarket, shop, or deli. I'd be ashamed—like I am about that highlighter pen today.

It happened so easily and so quickly. I was fingering it, and suddenly it was in my pocket. Then my heart started thumping so hard I thought everyone could hear it. I flushed on the inside and felt terrible, so I quickly put it back. But I still feel guilty of stealing.

Sorry, Jesus. I try, but it is so hard to be honest—especially when things are put there so easy to take. Make me strong, so that I am honest for the right reasons, and not just because I'm scared of getting caught. Make me caring for the things of others. And forgive me for all the times I have failed. Amen.

Music's Magic!

Turn it down! Do you have to have it so loud? We can't hear ourselves think!" is what the adults say. But that's how I love it! You can't hold back music—that rhythm, that beat, that excitement, that action!

But it's such a pity: Sometimes such crude or suggestive words go with catchy music, and I feel let down; it's hard to own the music when your faith won't let you own the words. And it's just as bad when your favorite singers live such loose, ungodly lives.

Thank you, Lord, for music, for its pleasure and entertainment. For all music, from rock to classics. Help me to enjoy it, except for when it is a bad influence—and I know when that is. Help me, too, to sing heartily of you and your love, my Lord and my God. Amen.

HANG-UP ABOUT HANDICAPS

They said that she had to have her leg amputated, cut off, just above the knee. Cancer, they said—and only fifteen! So she had to deal with something I don't like thinking about: having a handicap for life.

I'm so grateful that it's not me. But what if it were? How strange would I look? Would people stare? Would people pull away from me? Would I still have friends? What fun could I have—apart from wheelchair sports? A permanent disability is scary.

Jesus, thank you for my healthy body. Please help me to treat it with proper care, and protect me from permanent injury. Forgive me for my hang-ups about disabled people; it's because I'm scared of what I don't understand, and of ending up like them. Help me to treat them with kindness and caring love, and to support their courage and determination—as you do. Amen.

So much garbage

Mine is lime-green; when it's not knocked over, it stands so helpfully in the corner of my bedroom. Most of the time, it varies between full and overflowing—full of wadded-up paper, candy wrappers, bus tickets, fluff, cotton balls, tissues, pencil shavings, fingernail clippings, and so forth. If they're broken, used up, dirtied, discarded, or have no set place, into my personal garbage can they go.

Life is so full of disposable things—cans, cartons, bottles, plastic bags, sticks, tubes, wrappers. So many things we can use and throw away without a care.

Jesus, don't let me build my life around temporary things, but around things with concrete, lasting value: truth, respect, self-discipline, honesty, forgiveness, compassion. Above all, through your Holy Spirit, give me faith, hope, and love, my Savior and Lord. Amen.

Hassles about smoking

Some of the others at school say it's cool to smoke. I saw them at it again on the way home. One had the butt pinched professionally between pale lips; another held hers hanging limp from what was clearly a well-practiced hand.

Of course, why be surprised—when magazine ads show tanned skin on slim and trim bodies, energy, action, and sophistication all wrapped in one beautiful package. Yes, it all looks cool.

No, not all! There are the warnings: "Smoking Is a Health Hazard," and from my parents: "Smoke and you're dead!"

It's strange how the things that are considered cool give me the greatest hassles. It mostly seems that I want to choose what's wrong/bad in preference to what's right/good—and that the things on the cool side end up on the wrong side. I've got to the stage where I agree smoking is unwise, but I'm still not sure if it's wrong.

Lord, help me to sort all this out and to make a wise choice. Help me to be informed—especially by using the Bible. When the answers are not clear-cut, bring me along the path that ends up with an understanding of your will. Amen.

Always alive

I wonder how many others have been torturing themselves like I have? When I have taken time to think about my real, long-term future, I've often got scared by the thoughts popping up in my mind. Will I go to heaven when I die—can I really be sure? What if I have a heart attack and die just when I'm angry and speaking wrong things? What if I die one day after having forgotten to (or not having time to) pray to God for forgiveness? Will my faith be big enough or good enough at the moment I die?

Thank goodness, that torture is now over; I am happy and at peace—thanks to my pastor's devotion tonight. He explained that believers in Jesus are in "a state of grace," an ongoing condition of forgiveness and salvation. My future does not rest on my faith, but on what faith takes hold of. It does not depend on how strong my faith is, or what sin I might be doing at the moment of death, but on God's grace in Jesus which faith clings to.

Thank you, Lord, for gospel-preachers like my pastor, and for the marvelous certainty of your gospel-promises. From now on I will cling to your beautiful promise: "Do not be afraid, little flock [that includes me!], for your

Father has been pleased to give you the kingdom" (Luke 12:32 NIV). Wow! I have been given eternal life already—now, today, not just when I die. Now I can really live! Amen.

"Remember your Creator while you are still young." (Ecclesiastes 12:1 TEV)